# INTERPRETING THE OLD TESTAMENT

*A Century of the Oriel Professorship*

BY

ERNEST NICHOLSON

ORIEL PROFESSOR OF THE
INTERPRETATION OF
HOLY SCRIPTURE

*An Inaugural Lecture*

DELIVERED BEFORE THE UNIVERSITY OF OXFORD
ON 3 FEBRUARY 1981

CLARENDON PRESS · OXFORD
1981

Oxford University Press, Walton Street, Oxford OX2 6DP
London Glasgow New York Toronto
Delhi Bombay Calcutta Madras Karachi
Kuala Lumpur Singapore Hong Kong Tokyo
Nairobi Dar es Salaam Cape Town
Melbourne Auckland
and associate companies in
Beirut Berlin Ibadan Mexico City

Published in the United States by
Oxford University Press, New York

© Ernest Nicholson 1981

All rights reserved. No part of this publication may be reproduced,
stored in a retrieval system, or transmitted, in any form or by any means,
electronic, mechanical, photocopying, recording, or otherwise, without
the prior permission of Oxford University Press

This book is sold subject to the condition that it shall not, by way of trade or otherwise, be lent,
re-sold, hired out, or otherwise circulated without the publisher's prior consent in any form of
binding or cover other than that in which it is published and without a similar condition
including this condition being imposed on the subsequent purchaser

British Library Cataloguing in Publication Data
Nicholson, Ernest
Interpreting the Old Testament
1. Bible. O.T. – Hermeneutics – Addresses, essays, lectures
I. Title
221.6'01    BS476
ISBN 0-19-951533-6

Printed in Great Britain
by S & S Press
Oxford

# INTERPRETING THE OLD TESTAMENT
# A CENTURY OF THE
# ORIEL PROFESSORSHIP

I

Mr Vice-Chancellor, the Statute for the foundation of the Oriel Professorship of the Interpretation of Holy Scripture was published one hundred years ago this term. The Professorship owes its foundation to the University Commission of 1877. A few years earlier each Board of Studies had been asked by the Hebdomadal Council to submit a report of what it considered its needs to be, including especially any requirement for additional teaching appointments. Writing on behalf of the School of Theology, the Regius Professor of Divinity, J. B. Mozley, stated that the Board of Studies considered the existing theology professoriate sufficient for the needs of the School: '[the] existing chairs', he wrote, 'practically provide for the languages and interpretation of the Old and New Testament, for Doctrine, for Ecclesiastical and Patristic Theology, for Liturgies as included in Pastoral Theology, and for Apologetics.'[1] The only modest qualification to this was contained in an accompanying letter from H. P. Liddon, Dean Ireland's Professor of Exegesis, asking for an assistant teacher for his chair.[2] Such a request did not arise in the case of the other chairs in the Faculty, the canon professorships at Christ Church, each of which at that time realized an annual income of £1,500 from which their holders were able to provide for such

[1]*Statement of the Requirements of the University adopted by the Hebdomadal Council on the 19th of March 1877, with the Papers upon which it was founded*, Oxford 1877, pp. 64ff.
[2]Ibid., p. 70.

additional teaching as they deemed necessary. But the endowment of the Dean Ireland's chair, which was unattached to any canonry, realized an annual income far short of this at little more than £300. Liddon himself had been appointed to a canonry at St. Paul's in 1870 quite independently of his appointment that same year to the Dean Ireland's Professorship. He was, in addition, a Student of Christ Church. From his combined sources of income he had been providing for additional teaching for his chair and continued to do so; throughout his tenure he employed John Wordsworth except for a short period when the young Charles Gore was his assistant.[3] But in order that such an arrangement could be guaranteed for his successors Liddon now asked that the appointment of a permanent Assistant Lecturer for his chair be considered.

The thought may have occurred to you, Mr Vice-Chancellor, that these stated requirements of the School of Theology were uncharacteristically timid. Let me therefore say immediately that they were short-lived. This report of the School's Board of Studies was submitted to the Hebdomadal Council in November 1873, just three years after the establishment of the Honour School of Theology, and the intervening time, as Pusey later stated to the Commission, had been insufficient to enable the Board to assess properly what the needs of the new School were likely to be.[4] Hence, by 1877, when the Commission began taking oral evidence, Liddon's unpretentious request had become rather more ambitious, and he, supported by Pusey and Wordsworth, now asked for the establishment of a Professorship of the Interpretation of Holy Scripture.

In asking for this new chair Liddon now stated, quite contrary to Mozley's report of a few years earlier, that there was 'no sufficient provision in the divinity faculty for the

[3]See E. W. Watson, *Life of Bishop John Wordsworth*, London 1915, p. 76.
[4]*University of Oxford Commission. Part I. Minutes of Evidence Taken By the Commissioners, Together With An Appendix and Index*, London 1881, p. 295, no. 4578 (cited hereafter as *Commission*).

interpretation of Scripture'.[5] He spoke of the fundamental importance of the study of the Bible in a faculty of theology and, under the venerable maxim *bonus textuarius, bonus theologus*, of the necessity of discovering as far as possible the exact meaning of its original text as the first and most important step towards a knowledge of revealed religion. For this, he reminded the Commissioners, there had been an abundant increase of materials in recent years, though, true to his own Tractarian convictions, he added: 'The area of our religious knowledge, as we believe, does not admit of additions; it is what it was in the first age of the Church. But our means of arriving at the exact sense of the sacred text are constantly improving.'[6]

He spoke also of the necessity to consider 'the great activity of foreign theologians', especially those who represented what he termed 'the negative criticism'. He was referring to the Tübingen school of New Testament criticism under the leadership of F. C. Baur: 'Thirty years ago in Oxford', he said, 'few people had an acquaintance with the vast literature which has been created by the later School of Tübingen. Now all our able men who study theology at all have, at least, a general notion of the drift of the speculations of Baur, Zeller, and Hilgenfeld. It is impossible for any Professor of the Interpretation of the New Testament to ignore these and kindred speculations.'[7] Baur's work on St. Paul had greatly appealed to Benjamin Jowett.[8] But Liddon described the Tübingen School as a 'desolate waste'[9] and what he had in mind was of course the defence of orthodoxy against the claims of such 'negative criticism', and such a defence appears to have been a prevailing characteristic of New Testament teaching in the faculty at that time.[10]

[5] Ibid., p. 292, no. 4544.
[6] Ibid., p. 290, no. 4537.
[7] Ibid., p. 290, no. 4537.
[8] E. Abbot and L. Campbell, *Life and Letters of Benjamin Jowett*, London 1897, vol. I, p. 142.
[9] R. E. Prothero, *The Life and Correspondence of A. P. Stanley*, London 1893, vol. II, p. 169.
[10] See O. Chadwick, *The Victorian Church*, Part II, London 1970, pp. 68f.

The increasing discoveries of archaeology, and especially the deciphering of cuneiform inscriptions, Assyriology, must also claim the close attention of the new professor, Liddon told the Commissioners. 'To this must be added', he went on, 'the whole group of questions which are connected with the earlier portions of Genesis, such as the relation of the Mosaic cosmogony and the early history of man, as described in Scripture, to the more recent results of physical science. For dealing with these grave questions, a Professor of Biblical Interpretation is responsible.'[11]

Coming to his specific proposal, Liddon urged the creation of a new Regius Professorship of the Interpretation of Holy Scripture which would be endowed with a canonry at Christ Church. At this point, incidentally, Liddon's evidence to the Commissioners provides the answer to a question which is still often asked today and to which sometimes answers of a rather fanciful nature concerning biblical hermeneutics are offered, namely, why the chair which was eventually established bears in its title the term 'Interpretation' whilst the Dean Ireland's professorship is of 'Exegesis'. No mystique was attached to this difference in terminology, certainly not originally: 'I should propose to call him (it is a trifle, but it is better to mention it)', Liddon said to the Commissioners, 'the Regius Professor of the *Interpretation* of Holy Scripture rather than Exegesis. People write to me from the country to ask me what Exegesis means, and it is better to call a professor by a name which will describe his work as plainly as may be.'[12]

As to how the new chair was to be financed, Liddon's suggestion, which he had evidently discussed with Pusey, was that the income of four of the canon professorships should be reduced, on their next vacancies, from £1,500 to £1,250 per year and the surplus which would thus accrue used to provide an income of £1,000 per year for the new professorship. Out of

[11]*Commission*, p. 290, no. 4537.
[12]Ibid., p. 291, no. 4538.

INTERPRETING THE OLD TESTAMENT 7

gratitude to Dean Ireland, the chair bearing his name, or perhaps a readership, should continue, but should be subordinated to the new Regius Professorship and its duties more definitely prescribed.

Liddon anticipated a possible counter-suggestion to his proposal, that is, that the existing deficiency in the faculty of which he spoke might be satisfied if the Dean Ireland's chair were permanently endowed with a canonry at Rochester Cathedral and thus placed upon a new and financially more secure basis. The canonry in question had been annexed by Queen Anne in 1714 to the Provostship of Oriel College and was currently held by Provost Hawkins. Since, however, the Provostship had now been secularized, the Universities of Oxford and Cambridge Act of 1877, in a clause evidently slipped in at the last moment, made provision that the Commissioners might use the canonry on its next vacancy and, with the concurrence of the Ecclesiastical Commissioners, 'provide that such canonry shall be thenceforth permanently annexed and united to some office or place of theological or ecclesiastical character in or connected with the University of Oxford'. Liddon considered such a possibility concerning the future of his own chair only second best: 'Speaking in this matter from experience', he stated, 'I should say that a second and distant centre is not really favourable to the sustained and concentrated work which is wanted. If nothing better can be done for the subject, this arrangement will be hereafter an improvement on the present provisions for the subject. But it is desirable that the professor of the interpretation of holy scripture should be endowed here in Oxford with an Oxford Canonry.'[13]

If I may digress somewhat for a moment here, this proposal for a new chair of Biblical Interpretation was not the only one that Liddon now ventured to set before the Commissioners. He also suggested the foundation of a Professorship of Canon Law,

[13] Ibid., p. 292, no. 4548.

which might be held by a layman, a Professorship of Christian Ethics and a Professorship or Readership in Liturgies. He also proposed that one of the two Arabic chairs then in the University might be appropriated to the study of Syriac and that an appointment in Rabbinical Hebrew should also be considered. The faculty's tame report of 1873 was thus left even further behind. In this, however, the School of Theology was pursuing a course by no means unrepresented in the case of other Schools at that time. Law, for example, in 1873 asked for two additional chairs, increased this a year later to four or five, and subsequently to a firm six. History in 1873 requested two additional chairs, one in English History and one in English Literature, but by 1876 this had been increased with further requests for a Professor of 'Foreign History', a Professor of Church History, one in Indian History, and one in 'Northern Antiquities', though the redoubtable Dr Stubbs, Regius Professor of Modern History, dissented from some of these ambitious designs and was particularly averse to the foundation of a chair of English Literature in the History Faculty, declaring to the Commissioners: 'I think that to have the History School hampered with *dilettante* teaching, such as the teaching of English literature, must necessarily do great harm to the school.'[14] He was of course echoing a widespread prejudice of the day—Cambridge knew it also—against the teaching of English Literature in the University. Happily, however, the Commissioners did not share the prejudice and founded, by a Statute approved in 1882, the Merton Professorship of English Language and Literature.

Several witnesses urged upon the Commissioners the necessity for a second chair of Hebrew. Most notable among these was T. K. Cheyne, then a Fellow of Balliol and later to become Oriel Professor. He argued that the existing Regius Professorship of Hebrew was inadequate on the grounds that the exegesis it was expected to provide was 'practically limited

[14]Ibid., p. 75, no. 1234.

# INTERPRETING THE OLD TESTAMENT

to the *exegesis* recognised by the Anglican Church'; 'it is desirable', he told the Commissioners, 'that there should be a professor who should treat of the *exegesis* from a purely philological point of view, that is to say, that he should give the external sense as the laws of the language required.'[15] Cheyne was unable to persuade the Commissioners that his notion of such a professor was not simplistic: 'By what possible mode of electing a professor', they asked him, 'would you avoid his presenting his own point of view, whether it was religious or anti-religious?' A few days later Pusey, the Regius Professor of Hebrew, supported their scepticism: 'If the lecturer were anti-theological,' he told them, 'he would have a bias one way, and if he were theological he might have a bias the other way, but you cannot avoid it.'[16] This of course was just as much an oversimplification as Cheyne's view, and we are probably not incorrect in seeing in all this a certain amount of shadow-boxing. What Cheyne really desired and what Pusey just as much dreaded was an historico-critical interpretation of the Bible, and the essential difference between the two points of view was not between theological and anti-theological exegesis but between an interpretative tradition which was becoming outmoded and one which was already rejoicing in the dawning of its day, perhaps over-confident that all would be gain without any losses.

I shall outline the rise and nature of the new method later, but let me now return to the outcome of Liddon's petition for the establishment of a Regius Professorship of the Interpretation of Holy Scripture. In this he was strongly supported, as I have already said, by the influential voices of Pusey and Wordsworth. But the Commissioners were apparently unwilling to establish another canon professorship at Christ Church. There may have been several reasons for this. Christ Church during the 1850s and 1860s had undergone its

[15] Ibid., p. 230, nos. 3746ff.
[16] Ibid., p. 296, no. 4580.

own internal troubles, and it is possible that the Commissioners did not wish to disturb at this stage the delicate balance which had been arrived at concerning the relationship between the Canons and the Students in the government of the College.[17] Or again, of the six canonries now remaining no fewer than five were also attached to professorships and the Commissioners may have considered it undesirable to add further to these. But the most obvious reason was probably that the canonry at Rochester offered a ready solution to Liddon's proposal. Notwithstanding his stated preference, the handwritten minutes of the Commission, in an entry for 11 November 1879, record a draft statute for uniting the canonry with the Dean Ireland's chair. This proposal was, however, abandoned, for reasons which I have been unable to discover; there is no further reference to it in the minutes. The first reference to the Oriel Professorship is contained in the minutes for 10 February 1881 and on 15 March that year a proposed statute for its foundation was published in the University Gazette. There was no opposition to it and it was sealed by the Commission on 26 April and by the Ecclesiastical Commissioners two days later. It was approved by the Queen in Council in May of the following year. The chair was to be called 'The Oriel Professorship of the Interpretation of Holy Scripture' to which was to be annexed and united, when it next fell vacant, the canonry at Rochester.[18]

In November 1882 Provost Hawkins died at Rochester and the canonry became immediately annexed to the newly founded chair. It was advertised in January 1883 and John Wordsworth, much to the delight of Liddon, was elected in March of that year.

---

[17]See E. G. W. Bill and J. F. A. Mason, *Christ Church and Reform 1850–1867*, Oxford 1970.
[18]The canonry was separated from the chair in 1950 after the retirement of D. C. Simpson.

## II

This addition to the Theology School's professoriate was the third significant change to have taken place within a few months. In the preceding September Pusey had died and some days later Liddon resigned his chair to devote himself to writing the life of his great friend. In October S. R. Driver was invited by Mr Gladstone on behalf of the Queen to become Regius Professor of Hebrew, and in December William Sanday was elected to the Dean Ireland's chair. Both men were of a different temperament and mould from either of their respective predecessors and both were already known to favour, though in a cautious and moderate manner, the new critical learning which Pusey and Liddon had so ardently rejected. Wordsworth, on the other hand, had been the close ally of Pusey and Liddon and continued throughout his life to maintain a considerable reserve towards the deeper issues of biblical criticism. Yet the contribution of Wordsworth, whom Sanday later described as amongst the most learned Oxford men of the nineteenth century,[19] was in every way as lasting as anything produced by either Sanday or Driver. This was his critical edition of the Vulgate New Testament, the work by which, at least in the field of biblical studies, his name remains remembered. Plans for it had been drawn up in 1878 and in 1882 he had published a draft scheme for it, which he revised shortly after his appointment to the Oriel chair. On becoming Bishop of Salisbury in 1885 he engaged the partnership of H. J. White for the continuation of the work which is still usually referred to as 'Wordsworth and White'. But though White's contribution was both essential and invaluable, Sanday recorded correctly that by the time White joined in the labours 'the whole plan of the work was already settled and already had imprinted upon it the individual stamp of its first progenitor.'[20]

[19] In his Memorial of Bishop Wordsworth in *Proceedings of the British Academy*, V, 1911–12, p. 533.
[20] Ibid., p. 540.

It would be impossible here to give any adequate indication of the quality and importance of this work. It was as near exhaustive as was possible: 'the chief editor from the first followed his bent', Sanday recorded, 'and the consequence is that his work—if not exhaustive—is nevertheless a striking monument of the wealth of detail, textual, historical, and illustrative, that could be brought together by a single hand.' As I have said, the work is often referred to as 'Wordsworth and White'. But it is a title which requires a significant extension, for what the combined labours of these two left unfinished was brought to an eminent completion by one of Wordsworth's distinguished successors in the Oriel chair, Dr H. F. D. Sparks. So permit a successor of Dr Sparks to correct that title to 'Wordsworth, White and Sparks'. I need only add that their edition of the Vulgate New Testament played a major role in the recent Stuttgart edition of the Vulgate Bible to which also Professor Sparks was a pre-eminent contributor.[21]

By the time Wordsworth was leaving for Salisbury in 1885 a change had already taken place in the theological climate at Oxford and an increasing number of the younger minds were now espousing the new critical methods and ideas. Already in 1884 Liddon, in a letter to Henry Scott Holland, wrote: 'I have feared sometimes that the younger Churchmanship of Oxford was undergoing a silent but very serious change through its eagerness to meet modern difficulties and its facile adoption of new intellectual methods.'[22] No doubt he had primarily in mind some of his younger Tractarian colleagues who just a few years later were to produce *Lux Mundi* (1889) which so greatly shocked and saddened him. But it is not unlikely that he included S. R. Driver whose appointment as Regius Professor of Hebrew he had not favoured, preferring instead the noted Assyriologist A. H. Sayce whom Pusey had also evidently

---

[21] *Biblia Sacra Iuxta Vulgatam Versionem*, Württembergische Bibelanstalt, Stuttgart 1969.
[22] S. Paget (ed.), *H. S. Holland, Memoir and Letters*, London 1921, p. 112.

# INTERPRETING THE OLD TESTAMENT 13

thought of as his successor.[23] Both regarded Sayce as a 'safe' man and indeed as time went by he was more and more seen as a champion of orthodoxy against the rising tide of critical views in Old Testament study. Driver on the other hand showed early signs of being won to the new critical views, especially those of Julius Wellhausen whose major work on the history of Israel, preceded by his famous analysis of the Pentateuch, had appeared in the 1870s.[24] Of Wellhausen's *Prolegomena to the History of Israel* Liddon wrote: 'I have read Wellhausen, and have a robust confidence that he will go the way of other Rationalists before him.'[25] But Driver's interest in Wellhausen was no passing flirtation and from the early 1880s onwards he sought in characteristically thorough manner to verify the critical foundations of Wellhausen's work, especially with regard to the analysis of the Pentateuch, and published his results in his *Introduction to the Literature of the Old Testament* which appeared in 1891 and which remains the most thorough work of its kind ever published by a British Old Testament scholar.

That Pusey was succeeded by Driver was indeed a sign that the old order had passed. That Wordsworth was succeeded in 1885 by T. K. Cheyne was an even greater indication, for Cheyne, very much more than Driver at that time and always very much more aggressively, had long since committed himself whole-heartedly to the new methods in the study of the Old Testament. His evidence to the Commission which I mentioned earlier gives a sign of this, but as early as 1873 he had declared that the most important results of Colenso's work on the Pentateuch as also of recent German research, notably that of Graf which became so fundamental for Wellhausen's work, would be confirmed.[26]

[23] See A. H. Sayce, *Reminiscences*, London 1923, pp. 213ff.
[24] The analysis of the Pentateuch was first published as a series of articles in *Jahrbücher für Deutsche Theologie* 1876 and 1877 and was subsequently published as *Die Composition des Hexateuchs und der historischen Bücher des Alten Testaments*, Berlin 1885. His *Geschichte Israels I* appeared in Berlin 1878 and in subsequent editions as *Prolegomena zur Geschichte Israels*. It was translated into English 1885.
[25] See J. O. Johnston, *Life and Letters of Henry Parry Liddon*, London 1904, p. 361.
[26] *The Academy*, iv, 1873, pp. 85–7.

In temperament Driver and Cheyne were contrasting figures. Driver: reserved, painstakingly exact and cautious in weighing evidence; patient—too patient at times for Cheyne's liking[27]—and above all devout in his approach, one of whom it was said that 'he taught the faithful criticism, and the critics faith'.[28] Cheyne: just as widely learned, but somewhat abrasive—one senses that his evidence to the Commissioners was a trifle irritating—frequently impatient and with a tendency to want to shock; he lacked Driver's fine sense of balance and indeed became more unbalanced with the years and completely so from around the turn of the century after which his work became increasingly eccentric and even bizarre. But before that sad change he shared with Driver an apparently unbounded energy and although they both had notable predecessors amongst British scholars, especially William Robertson Smith who powerfully influenced both of them, it is to them more than to any other that the modern study of the Old Testament in England owes its foundation.

### III

'The modern study of the Old Testament'—what did this mean? Cheyne, you will recall, spoke to the Commissioners in 1877 of the necessity of giving the 'external sense' of the biblical text as the laws of the language require, that is, of an exegesis free of any *a priori* doctrinal or confessional commitment on the part of the interpreter. What he had in mind had been more expansively expressed by Jowett in his famous essay in *Essays and Reviews* in 1860,[29] an essay which, as far as British biblical scholarship was concerned, brought the interpretative method in question to the forefront of discussion. 'Interpret the

---

[27]Cheyne's appreciation and criticisms of Driver's work are contained in his *Founders of Old Testament Criticism*, London 1893, chs. 11, 12, 13.
[28]The quotation comes from the entry on S. R. Driver in the *Dictionary of National Biography*.
[29]London 1860, pp. 330–433.

Scripture like any other book', he wrote. 'The first step is to know the meaning, and this can only be done in the same careful and impartial way that we ascertain the meaning of Sophocles or of Plato.'[30] Jowett thus stated one of the cardinal principles of the method, namely, that any given biblical text has but one meaning, the meaning which the original author intended for those to whom he addressed himself in his own historical situation: 'No other science of Hermeneutics is possible', he wrote, 'but an inductive one, that is to say, one based on the language and thoughts and narrations of the sacred writers.'[31] It thus demands a historical approach and the cultivation of an empathy with the author in his own ancient context: 'It is the business of the interpreter to place himself as nearly as possible in the position of the sacred writer.'[32] It was historical also in that the concept of development is necessitated when dealing with a library of books such as the Bible contains from very varied ages and periods: 'Each writer, each successive age, has characteristics of its own.'[33]

What Jowett was describing was the historico-critical method which had emerged and developed largely in Germany during the century or so before he wrote. It was historical in its analysis and dating of the sources, in its attempt to determine their meaning and evaluate their reliability, and in seeking to arrange them so as to uncover the origin and development of the religious and theological ideas which they embody and express. It was, in short, a thoroughgoing historical hermeneutics, and it was this which gradually came to govern nineteenth-century biblical interpretation and which has continued to do so in the twentieth century.

It is only within the past few years that the supremacy of this history-oriented hermeneutics in Old Testament study has been challenged and a new debate on hermeneutics currently

[30] Ibid., p. 377.
[31] Ibid., p. 378.
[32] Ibid., p. 378.
[33] Ibid., p. 382.

engages the attention of scholars. I shall mention something more of this later, though of necessity only briefly so. But in order to gain a clearer perspective on this current discussion, let me say something more at this stage about the historico-critical method. Its very name provides the key to its primary intellectual foundations and principles: it took its rise with and one might almost say its mandate from the historical thinking and understanding which began to emerge in the period of the Enlightenment, received vital impulses from Romanticism, and burgeoned in the German historical school of the nineteenth century.[34] To a remarkable extent, indeed to a greater extent than has often been realized or acknowledged, it was this historical thinking that provided the basis of biblical hermeneutics in the nineteenth century, and more than the theologians and biblical scholars themselves it was the leading figures of the German historical school—Barthold Gustav Niebuhr, Wilhelm von Humboldt, Leopold von Ranke, Johann Gustav Droysen, Theodor Mommsen, and others—who created the interpretative framework and provided the method. Historical thinking and understanding, its *Fragestellung*, became the way of biblical interpretation. Thus W. M. L. deWette, one of the founders of modern Old Testament study, early in the nineteenth century could write that 'the general laws of (biblical) hermeneutics are also those of historical interpretation' (*Die allgemeinen Gesetzte der Hermeneutik sind auch die der historischen Interpretation*).[35]

The full working out of this historical interpretative method in Old Testament study did not of course take place at a stroke; it too had a history and a development. It by no means reached its culmination in the work of Wellhausen, though his

---

[34]From the many studies describing the rise of historical thinking and the historical movement in Germany may be selected, for example, the lucid presentation by G. G. Iggers, *The German Concept of History: The National Tradition of Historical Thought from Herder to the Present*, Middletown 1968.
[35]W. M. L. deWette, *Beiträge zur Einleitung in das Alte Testament*, vol. 2, Halle 1806–7, p.3.

achievements were certainly a landmark in its progress.[36] Within a few years of the publication of his *Prolegomena*, and at the very time that Driver and Cheyne were labouring here for a wider acceptance of historico-critical exegesis, this method advanced to a new and still more thoroughgoing historical stage. This new stage was achieved by the so-called 'history-of-religions' school or movement whose pioneering figure, in the field of Old Testament study, was Hermann Gunkel.[37] It is a further indication of the close relationship between this Old Testament interpretative method and the historiographical tradition to which I have referred that this fresh movement in biblical studies accompanied and reflected a revitalization and re-evaluation of historical thinking which emerged in the last decade or so of the nineteenth century. We must not of course over-schematize in our description of this period, but briefly, and at the risk of some over-simplification, it may be said that these years saw the re-assertion of the autonomy and peculiar nature of the cultural sciences (*Geisteswissenschaften*) over against what were seen as the increasingly imperialistic claims of the natural sciences (*Naturwissenschaften*) to provide the means of comprehending not only the physical sciences proper but all phenomena of human life and experience.[38] Positivism, materialism, naturalism, any 'mechanistic' approach to understanding historical and cultural developments were identified as the enemies, and the counter movements once more drew upon the Idealist and Romantic traditions. The leaders of the 'history-of-religions' movement self-consciously identified themselves with this revitalization in historical

[36]For the influence of the historical movement upon Wellhausen see especially L. Perlitt, *Wallhausen und Vatke: Geschichtesphilosophische Voraussetzungen und historiographische Motive für die Darstellung der Religion und Geschichte Israels durch Wilhelm Vatke und Julius Wellhausen* (BZAW 94), Berlin 1965.
[37]See W. Klatt, *Hermann Gunkel. Zu einer Theologie der Religionsgeschichte und zur Entstehung der formgeschichtlichen Methode* (FRLANT 100), Göttingen 1969. The rise of the 'history-of-religions' movement is described in H. Gressmann, *Albert Eichhorn und die Religionsgeschichtliche Schule*, Göttingen 1914.
[38]For a recent and lucid treatment of this see especially M. Ermarth, *Wilhelm Dilthey: The Critique of Historical Reason*, Chicago and London 1978.

thinking and more than ever exemplified in their work the Idealist and Romantic traditions, particularly as these had governed the development of the classical period of the German history movement in the nineteenth century.[39] Thus Gunkel, writing a century or so after deWette's statement which I quoted a moment ago, could describe this new surge forward in historical exegesis as 'nothing other than a new wave of the powerful historical current which has flowed from our great idealist thinkers and poets over our entire cultural life and long since into our theology' (*In Wirklichkeit ist sie* [*die religionsgeschichtliche Bewegung*] *nicht anderes als eine neue Welle des gewaltigen geschichtlichen Stromes, der sich von unseren grossen idealistischen Denkern und Dichtern her über unser gesamtes Geistesleben und auch seit lange in unsere Theologie ergossen hat*).[40]

Negatively, the effects of this can be seen in, for example, the way in which the scholars of this new movement viewed the purely literary-critical approach of their immediate predecessors, including most notably Wellhausen himself, as too 'mechanistic' and wooden; positively, the historical perspective was now further deepened by the development of form-criticism and traditio-historical research, by the attempt to penetrate behind the literature in its final form to discover the concrete sociological setting (*Sitz im Leben*) of each of the literary types, by a reappraisal of the creative role of ancient cultic life, by ascertaining the distinctiveness (*Eigentümlichkeit*) of Israelite religion among the religions of its ancient near eastern environment, and so forth.

Thus the development of historical exegesis in Old Testament studies virtually shadowed that of the nineteenth-century historiographical movement. What must be especially

---

[39]The close relationship between the 'history-of-religions' movement and this revitalization in historical thinking during the latter part of the nineteenth century has been perceptively described and documented by R. A. Oden in 'Hermeneutics and Historiography: Germany and America', *Seminar Papers: Society of Biblical Literature*, Chico 1980, pp. 135–57.
[40]H. Gunkel, 'Was will die "religionsgeschichtliche" Bewegung?', *Deutsch-Evangelisch* 5, 1914, 356f. Cf. W. Klatt, p. 26.

INTERPRETING THE OLD TESTAMENT 19

emphasized in all this, however, is that it was not merely a matter of biblical scholars adopting the particular techniques developed by the historiographical movement; much more fundamentally, it was believed that historical thinking provided the only valid and coherent hermeneutics for comprehending human phenomena. Thus, as brought to the zenith of its development by the 'history-of-religions' movement under the leadership of Gunkel, Gressmann and others, this hermeneutics was governed by the all-embracing principle that to understand a phenomenon such as that of Israelite religion was to understand its origin and growth, its 'becoming'.[41]

IV

Even a brief sketch such as this indicates the extent to which Old Testament interpretation came to be dominated by the categories and method of historical thinking. Given this, it was inevitable that the question of meaning in the biblical texts was to be answered in thoroughgoing historical terms, which is to say that meaning was believed to reside not in the text as such but in the data which can be adduced from the text concerning matters anterior or extrinsic to it. That is, the text itself was treated referentially. Thus, whole stretches of the Old Testament were analysed into their component and originally separate sources or literary strands which, having been arranged in chronological order, were then used for recovering the origin and development of Israel's sacral traditions, its religious beliefs and ideas, and so forth. For example, a narrative such as that of Exodus 1–15 was investigated for what it might yield concerning the historical events of the bondage and exodus from Egypt or about the nature and transmission of the traditions which developed around the original historical

[41]Gunkel himself stated this principle in just this way in 'The "Historical Movement" in the Study of Religion', *Expository Times* 38, 1926–7, p. 533. It is a direct echo of the eleventh of the twenty-four 'theses' laid down by Albert Eichhorn, the founder of the 'history-of-religions' movement. (See H. Gressmann, op. cit., p. 8.)

events. From a theological point of view it was then believed that the locus of revelation was in the events themselves—one thinks here of the 'mighty acts of God in history' type of theology—or in the traditions understood as credal confessions, or the like. Much of this remains of great value, but it has meant that the narrative itself has been regarded as of merely referential value; it has become nothing more than a source and it is as a source that it has its significance; the text itself is not a locus of revelation.

A sense of the loss of the importance of the final form of the biblical text was by no means unknown amongst earlier generations of Old Testament scholars. Thus, for example, G. von Rad, writing in 1938 after a period which had seen a proliferation of further source analysis as well as an increasing preoccupation with the pre-compositional stages in the growth of the literature of the Hexateuch, could speak of a weariness amongst scholars with a situation in which the final form of the text had come to be regarded as 'a starting point barely worthy of discussion, from which the debate should move away as rapidly as possible in order to reach the real problems underlying it'.[42] Yet not even von Rad's influential monograph stimulated a revival of concern with the Hexateuch in its final literary presentation, and in reality this monograph itself was almost exclusively concerned with only one of the various literary strata which the Hexateuch comprises, the so-called Yahwist document. It has been followed by many such studies, all focusing attention on the parts but not on the whole, whilst commentaries on the books of the Hexateuch have in general persisted in analysing each pericope into its separate literary strata as the only focus of exegesis without attempting any serious exposition of their final interconnected presentation.

Protest against such a fragmentation of the biblical literature

[42]G. von Rad, *Das formgeschichtliche Problem des Hexateuch*, BWANT IV:26, 1938 = *Gesammelte Studien zum Alten Testament*, München 1958, pp. 9–86. The quotation is from the English translation *The Problem of the Hexateuch and Other Essays*, Edinburgh and London, 1966, p. 1.

and against the predominantly referential handling of it characteristic of historical exegesis forms part of the background of the current renewed debate on hermeneutics in Old Testament study. Partly also it has its basis in a wider twentieth-century movement in hermeneutics. Influential, for example, has been Ferdinand de Saussure's work on linguistics, the principles of which have been eagerly taken up by various schools of structuralist analysis into the literary level itself. Or again, ideas first suggested by T. S. Eliot can be discerned.[43] The new directions in interpretation now being advocated are by no means identical, but they share a notable common goal which may be said to be to rediscover the significance of the final form of the text and to locate meaning at this level and not or not merely in what information it may yield concerning matters strictly extrinsic to it. If I may here call upon two words which are fast becoming a trifle overworked, they call for a synchronic reading of the text as against the diachronic handling of it which has characterized historical exegesis with its quest for sources, phases of redaction, and so forth.

Thus, for example, structural analysis seeks to rehabilitate the autonomy of the text as such and to find meaning in its forms and patterns; to use a phrase favoured in such circles, meaning is believed to be 'text-immanent'. Most notable among the new approaches being developed, however, and one upon which we may dwell a little, is that of the distinguished American scholar Brevard Childs, Professor of Old Testament at Yale University. Childs does not seek the abandonment of the historico-critical method but regards its usefulness as strictly limited. He calls instead for an exegesis which takes seriously the canonical context of each text. That is, exegesis of any given text should be directed to its place in the overall canon of scripture to which it belongs and its relationship with

---

[43]Especially his well known essay, first published in 1919, 'Tradition and the Individual Talent', reprinted in *Selected Prose*, Penguin Books, 1953, pp. 21ff.

other texts in the canon.[44] The emphasis is thus upon a synchronic reading of the text. Meaning is here located in the nature, shape, and use of the text as the scripture of the community of faith; there has been, it is maintained, a canonical shaping of the literature which transcends the original, historically contingent significance of a narrative, a prophetic oracle, a psalm, and so forth, and renders it valid for successive generations in the life and history of the community of faith. For example, historical exegesis has shown that the message of the prophet Amos, who lived in the eighth century B.C., was one of judgement without any announcement of renewal after judgement. Secondary additions to the book, largely at the end of chapter 9, have, however, given the book a message not merely of judgement but of hope beyond judgement. Wellhausen and earlier critics saw this shift from judgement to blessing as irreconcilable with the authentic message of the great prophet; it was, as Wellhausen himself put it, 'roses and lavender instead of blood and iron'.[45] For Childs, however, the 'effect of the canonical shaping of ch.9 is to place Amos's words of judgement within a larger theological framework, which, on the one hand, confirms the truth of Amos's prophecy of doom, and, on the other hand, encompasses it within the promise of God's will for hope and final redemption. In its canonically interpreted form the historically conditioned ministry of the eighth-century prophet of judgement serves as a truthful witness of scripture for the successive generations of Israel.'[46] Thus, by this means Israel was given in Amos's proclamation a 'prophetic word to serve continually against persistent and recurring abuses of religion which threaten true faith';[47] the arrangement of the material in the book as a whole by the use of editorial

[44]B. S. Childs, *Biblical Theology in Crisis*, Philadelphia 1970; *Introduction to the Old Testament as Scripture*, London 1979. His commentary on *Exodus*, London 1974, offers a detailed application of the principles he advocates.
[45]Cited by Childs, *Introduction*, p. 405 from J. Wellhausen, *Die kleinen Propheten übersetzt und erklärt*, 3rd edition, Berlin 1898, p. 96.
[46]Childs, p. 408.
[47]Ibid., p. 409.

commentary, hymnic doxology, and eschatological expansions has meant that the community of faith is continually confronted with 'the eternal God, the Creator and Redeemer of Israel, who was a living force both in the past, present, and future'.[48] Students of literature will know that modern developments in the quest for meaning in texts have by no means been without controversy and that the terrain to be traversed holds many a pitfall.[49] So too in biblical studies the debate is lively and the pitfalls manifold. What reaction to the various new trends now afoot ought to be encouraged? There are assuredly important fresh gains to be reaped from much that Childs and others are currently offering, not least of all from their insistence that exegesis must rediscover the significance of the final form of the text. Yet great caution is also essential here. It has been said, with some justification, that the history of our field of study resembles the labour of Sisyphus, that unfortunate king of Corinth whose fate in Hades was to roll a heavy stone up a high hill whence it promptly tumbled down to the bottom again, thus necessitating an eternal repetition of his sweated effort. It cannot seriously be considered, however, that such is to be our fate in the matter of hermeneutics, that the labours of many generations of historical exegesis have been a Sisyphean toil. I have time for but one example, but, I believe, a pertinent one in this context. It is one of a number of important observations made recently by my predecessor Professor Barr[50] and which I would put as follows. If in interpreting Old Testament texts we must, following Childs and others, develop a new sensitivity to the texts in their final form, we must now equally be on our guard against 'absolutizing' the final form, including its

[48]p. 410. Critical appraisals of Childs's approach by various scholars with a response by Childs are contained in *Journal for the Study of the Old Testament*, 16, 1980.
[49]See for example the lively discussion by E. D. Hirsch, *Validity in Interpretation*, New Haven and London, 1967 and *The Aims of Interpretation*, Chicago and London 1976.
[50]Especially his 'Historical Reading and the Theological Interpretation of Scripture', *Explorations in Theology* 7, London 1980, pp. 30–51. Cf. also his 'Story and History in Biblical Theology', *ibid.* pp. 1–17 (first published in *The Journal of Religion*, 56, 1976, pp. 1–17).

canonical context. That would be an impoverishment of our interpretative endeavours, for it is one of the richest gains of historical exegesis to have recovered earlier stages in the history of many such texts, that is, to have discerned the tradition-like nature of them; each individual stage must remain an object of reflection. To put the matter in theological terms, we must not regard the final form of the text, important as it is, as alone the locus of revelation, but remain sensitive to its earlier stages as also potentially revelatory. To fail to do so would be a frustration of the *spes hermeneutica*[51] no less than that which has in the past arisen from our preoccupation with the earlier stages at the expense of the final form of the text.

Mr Vice-Chancellor, I have mentioned the ill-fated Sisyphus, and I imagine that a Vice-Chancellor's nightmare of Hades is to have to listen to an inaugural lecture only to find on its completion and to all eternity that another which he has to attend is just beginning, especially if, as may be, many of them are to be delivered by theologians! Let me therefore hastily conclude. I seem to have come a long way from where I began this lecture, with Oxford in the 1870s and 1880s. But these concluding paragraphs point to a situation today not unlike that in which Liddon, Pusey, Jowett, Cheyne, and Driver lived and thought and worked, namely, a debate, not perhaps as heated as it was in those days, but a debate no less vigorous and challenging concerning a question which must engage the attention of a holder of the Oriel Professorship, the age-old question how we are to interpret the Old Testament.

---

[51] I have borrowed the phrase from F. Kermode's stimulating book *The Genesis of Secrecy: On the Interpretation of Narrative*, Cambridge Mass., and London, 1979.